THERE HAVE ALWAYS BEEN PUFFINS

by C.J. and Ba Rea

Bas Relief Publishing Group • Glenshaw, PA

Dedicated to
Sniglet,
Grandma and Grandpa
in honor of Beginnings, Completions
and Full Circles

Text © C.J. and Ba Rea 1997
Illustrations © Ba Rea 1997
All rights reserved
published by
Bas Relief Publishing Group, P.O Box 426, Glenshaw, PA 15116

ISBN 0-965-7472-0-4
Library of Congress Catalog Card Number 97-93621

Flying back to his burrow in the soft turf on top of Beehive One, Cid was amazed by a new development on the horned puffin ledge.

"Puffin chicks wearing glasses! Hmmm. Always did seem as though those horned puffins were a little short-sighted. I guess that goes along with being a ledge dweller. Now, with the silly puffin propaganda those humans are sending up here, the poor tikes are going to need ear plugs too."

There once was a puffin
and he didn't know nuffin.
He lived in the middle of
the deep
blue
sea.

It was a scene that Cid (veteran tufted puffin, Sydney L. Cirrhata) had watched all summer. The tour boat was full of humans. A naturalist on the bow of the boat was handing a microphone and a small book containing a variation of Florence Page Jaques' poem "There ONCE was a Puffin," to a young girl. The girl was to read the poem aloud as they passed through the active puffin breeding ground at the Beehive Islands.

"Humph," Cid thought. "I suppose it's good they take an interest in us. There's a lot we can teach them."

The **tufted puffin's** (*Lunda cirrhata*) breeding range is identical to the horned's range except that it continues southward to California and the Sea of Japan. In the winter, tufted puffins go farther out into the open ocean than the other two species. Tufted puffins have been seen 300 to 400 miles offshore in the Gulf of Alaska.

The **horned puffin's** (*Fratercula corniculata*) breeding range extends from the Chukchi Sea to Kurile Island in the southwest and Queen Charlotte Island in the southeast. In the winter they can be found on open water as far south as California.

and ⬜ Horned puffin winter and breeding ranges

and ⬜ Tufted puffin winter and breeding ranges

He ate little fishes which were most delicious, He had them for breakfast and he had them for tea.

But that poor little puffin he couldn't play nufffin, because he had no one to play with at all.

So he sat on his isle and he cried for a while. He felt very lonely and he felt very small.

Then along came those fishes and they said if you wishes you could have us for playmates instead of for tea.

As the weeks passed, the young horned puffins grew from fluffy feather balls to fine young puffin chicks. Tour boats motored under their ledges each day. The tourists could not see the chicks, but the chicks could see the boats and hear the story that was told about the puffins.

The **Atlantic puffin** (*Fratercula arctica*) covers territory from Labrador south to eastern Maine, eastward to Greenland, Iceland and Norway and south to the British Isles and northern France. They spend their winters at the edge of the pack ice in the North Atlantic away from the coast.

Puffins are members of the Alcidae or Auk family of diving birds. Alcids have wings which they use underwater for propulsion and in air for flight.

Atlantic puffin winter and breeding ranges

Now they all play together in all sorts of weather and the puffin eats yogurt like you and like me.

After six weeks on the ledges, the puffin chicks left. Fledging in the middle of the night, they took the puffin story with them out to the deep blue sea...

I'm just a puffin.
I know little or nuthin'.
I float every day on this
     sea,
         deep
             and blue.

I'm lonely and sad,
don't know right
     from bad.
I must make some
     fish friends,
         whatever
             I do.

"Fish friends?
HAH! He ate my Aunt Frieda just last night. I'd
like to take a bite out of his shoe size."

It had been several years since Cid had seen that bespectacled puffin chick, but he'd never forget those glasses. Dropping to the water he shouted, "For Pete's sake, eat the fish! I say there, young puffin, that song you're singing is a bunch of Homo sapien hogwash. You'll find a slippery friendship in fish, much better in the beak I'd say. What's your name, son?"

"I'm Al, sir, Al F. Corniculata, 'cept the fishes all call me Runenhide."

"Glad to meet you Al, and not a moment too soon, I might add. My name is Sydney L. Cirrhata but you can call me Cid. Al, that verse you are humming is rather misleading. Beware of humans and the rhymes that they read. The puffin version goes like this:"

Jaegers, gulls and peregrine falcons are puffin rivals and predators. Jaegers and gulls are most likely to act as pirates, stealing fish from puffin parents as they bring them to feed their chicks. The constant swirling mass of puffins over a rookery is a defense against this piracy and can also ward off the more direct attacks by peregrine falcons. In the Atlantic puffins' range, the great black-backed gull feeds on puffins. If the gulls begin a season preying on puffins, they will likely make them their sole food source.

POMARINE JAEGER

PEREGRINE FALCON

There have always been puffins. They're handsome and tough 'n' they float all winter on the deep blue seas.

They eat fishes all day, keeping warm in this way, with an eye to the sky for their winged enemies.

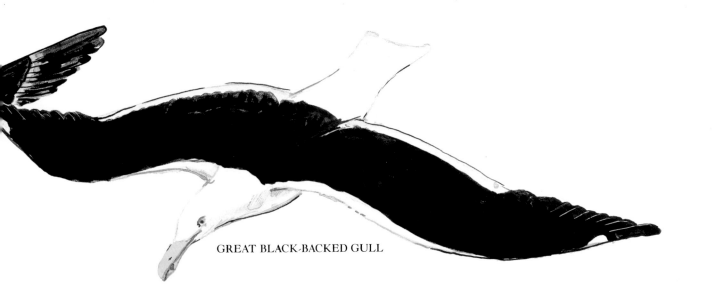

GREAT BLACK-BACKED GULL

The puffins' habit of becoming solitary for the winter serves as protection from their enemies. Jaegers and gulls prefer to follow large groups of migrating birds and seldom hassle solitary wintering puffins. The puffins' drab unobtrusive winter plumage and lack of beak plates make them difficult to spot for predators and birders alike.

TUFTED PUFFIN

HORNED PUFFIN

ATLANTIC PUFFIN

As Cid began the puffin version of the rhyme he was suddenly reminded of the time.
"Follow me lad...We need to leave for the rookery."
"The *rook-or-what?*" shouted Al, as he struggled to take off behind Cid.

As the spring days get longer,
puffin memories grow stronger.
They remember the others what fun it
     will
          be.

It takes many days
over oceans of waves,
to join friends and family at the
          old
               rookery.

"The rookery is where you visit all of your friends and relations each year."

"Cid, you mean I have friends and relations?" asked Al, out of breath from his attempts to keep up with the seasoned tufted puffin.

"Sure you do. Did you think you just crawled out from under that rock ledge?"

"Well, I did..."

"Nonsense! Haven't you been back yet? It's time! You've developed beautiful beak plates and, though I daresay a tuft is more elegant, that little horn above your eye is quite dashing. You're sure to find a mate."

The trip took several weeks. As Al and Cid approached the Beehive Islands, the air was alive with thousands of other puffins.

"Ah, there's my Alice," said Cid abruptly. "I'd know those tufts anywhere. I'll see you later Al. Good luck to you!"

"No, Cid! Wait... What should I do?"

They dress in their finery,
fit for winery and dinery,
impressing their mates with a dancing display.

With bright colors amazing,
their beaks are ablazing.
They court and cavort in exuberant play.

It is not known how puffins sense that it is time to return to their rookeries, but when the birds begin to come back it takes only a day or two for the entire colony to arrive. Puffins pair for life. As the birds arrive they gather in large flocks on the sea. Old pairs reunite and newcomers seek a mate.

Mating takes place on the water. The male puffin will signal the female puffin by nodding his beak, first holding it parallel to the water and then tipping it straight up in the air. The male will then make a short flight of about three feet to the female.

After mating one or both birds will wing-flap while remaining otherwise motionless on the water's surface.

A common display between mates is *billing*, in which puffins press or slap the lateral plates of their bills together. This display is often seen among horned puffins when one mate returns to the nest site.

In desperation Al halted and crashed into the water, nearly swamping a young horned puffin female.

"Hi! I remember you. You're Al. Remember me?...Cindy...the next ledge over...We fledged the same night."

After the great breeding celebration, like the horned puffins for generations past, Al and Cindy set their efforts to claiming and cleaning up a nesting site on the rocky ledge of Beehive One. High above, on the turfy top of the rocky island, tufted puffins like Cid and Alice prepared their burrows for nesting as well.

"Al, I didn't know it would be this hard to clean up our ledge."

Then off to the nest site
to clean it up just right,
digging and prying out
rocks and
debris.

After mating, puffins will stake out a nest site. Established pairs usually return to the same nest site each year. Tufted puffins and Atlantic puffins like to nest on soil and turf-covered islands or headlands where they dig a burrow up to six-and-a-half feet deep. The digging of a new burrow or the cleaning of a winter-ravaged burrow is done by both birds. They use their bills to pry loose rocks and debris and their feet to move soil.

At the end of their burrows, they construct a sparse nest of grasses and feathers.

Horned puffins nest on rocky slopes or ledges. They usually find well-sheltered spots that are tucked under rock overhangs.

Both tufted and Atlantic puffins defend their burrows and a small one to two foot area around the entrance. For Atlantic puffins, this territorial behavior extends to a take-off pad as well. Horned puffins are only territorial about their nest site and not the ledge nearby.

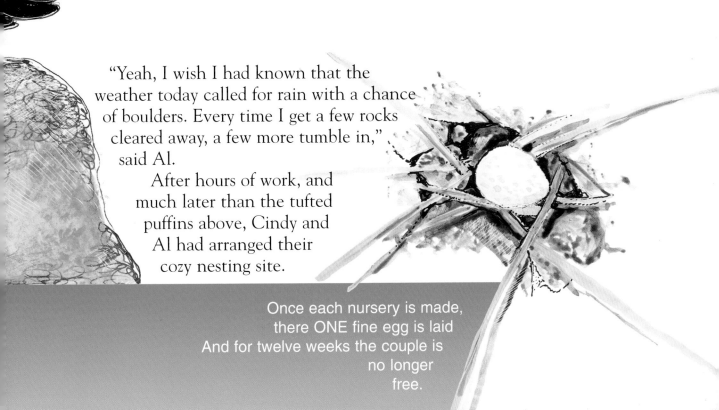

"Yeah, I wish I had known that the weather today called for rain with a chance of boulders. Every time I get a few rocks cleared away, a few more tumble in," said Al.

After hours of work, and much later than the tufted puffins above, Cindy and Al had arranged their cozy nesting site.

Once each nursery is made,
there ONE fine egg is laid
And for twelve weeks the couple is
no longer
free.

Puffins lay just one egg per year. If an egg is lost early enough in the season, they will lay a second egg to replace it. Both the male and the female birds spend time brooding to keep the egg warm.

During the incubation period both birds develop brood patches. These are areas with no feathers and an increased number of blood vessels which transfer heat from the parent to the egg. Puffins have two brood patches, one on either side of the breast bone under each wing. To incubate the egg they lean on it with one wing slightly lifted. When the chick has hatched and brooding is no longer necessary, feathers regrow on the parent's brood patches.

The length of incubation varies slightly for the three types of puffins. Tufted puffins sit on their eggs for as few as 30 days. Atlantic puffins take 42 days to hatch and horned puffins take about 38 days.

Upon hatching, the chick is a fuzzy ball of down. It is able to see and to move about the nest, but seems content to sit still and wait for its parent puffin to deliver fish.

Each bird takes a turn to keep the egg warm while the other returns for a meal from the sea.

Cid kept a close watch over the young horned puffin couple. They had laid their egg on the ledge and took turns brooding it. One morning he spotted Cindy looking worried and befuddled.

"Greetings Cindy. How's life on the ledge?"

"Oh Cid. It's good to see you. Al's at home keeping the egg warm. We're a little nervous though. Our egg is due to hatch any day and I just don't know how we're going to find enough fish for our chick."

"Have you ever been to a bait ball?"

"No. What's that?"

"Well, you don't need to get dressed up. Follow me. Let's go find one!"

"Excuse me. Pleased to meet you. My name is Al... uh, I mean Dad."

'Til the day they awake and they hear the egg break, and then, the real work begins for them all.

Cid guided Cindy to a tide rip area where he knew many birds kept watch for schools of feeding fish. As they approached, Cindy could not believe what she saw.

"Wait till you get a look under water," shouted Cid as he dove in.

Under the surface was a puffin's dream—a huge school of fish spreading in all directions.

"See, Cindy, there will be plenty of fish when your chick hatches."

Cindy, her mouth already full, mumbled cheerfully, "Mgh, grr right, dis is a blot of pish."

Murres, kittiwakes and puffins hit the waves by the dozens and together they search for a giant bait ball.

Serrated structures found inside the puffin's upper bill help them to gather many fish at a time.

Fishermen use the term bait ball to describe a school of small bait fish. In Alaska, capelin is a common bait fish. The school can be corralled by whales, bigger fish or diving birds. Seen from a boat, a bait ball looks like a flock of kittiwakes gathered on the surface of the water. The kittiwakes are the most visible participants because they do their fishing on the surface, gorging on fish that are trying to escape the birds underwater.

Cormorants are common bait ball participants. They are not alcids, but they swim under water using their webbed feet for paddles.

The alcids, common and thick billed murres, and tufted and horned puffins use their wings for propulsion and their feet to steer. Of all the bait ball participants, the murres can dive the deepest (over 300 feet). The cormorants stay closer to the surface at no more than one hundred foot depths. The puffins work hard to keep their buoyant bodies down as deep as 200 feet.

SAND LANCE

CAPELIN

Puffins often have a hard time flying after they have had a big meal. Individuals that use their wings both to swim and fly cannot weigh much more than two and a half pounds or their wings will not support their weight in the air.

They scoop up the fish
with a hope and a wish
that the babies will eat them and
grow big
and fat.

A puffin chick starts its life as down covered ball of fluff. It weighs about two-and-a-half ounces when it is born. In one month the chick increases its weight to eight times its birth weight. During the first three or four days of life, one of the parent puffins remains in the burrow with the chick.

After this period, the parents are rarely in the burrow unless they are feeding their young. A puffin nestling is fed two to five times a day. Fish are brought two to three at a time to the young puffin, and up to fourteen fish at a time as the chick nears fledging.

Al and Cindy's chick was a voracious eater, growing quickly into a strong young puffin.

"If you eat the rest of these fish that will be fourteen today! You've grown so fast!" said Cindy proudly.

Each chick is a dandy,
it eats fish like candy.
And Ma and Pa puffins are glad about
that.

Fledging occurs 38 to 52 days after hatching. The horned puffin seems to be the quickest to mature and leave the nest. When it is almost ready to fledge, the chick begins to spend some time at the burrow entrance, stretching its wings and taking in its surroundings. It was once thought that parents stopped feeding their young to encourage them to fledge and find food. However, scientists have also seen bewildered parents take food back to what has become an empty nest. No one is certain what causes the chick to fledge when it does.

Fledging occurs at night when danger from predators is decreased. An Atlantic puffin is able to fly to the water at fledging time. However, a tufted puffin is still flightless when it fledges. It must work its way down the slopes from its burrow, fluttering its wings for balance, not flight. Once in the water, the young puffin works its way out to sea where it spends the next three years.

For six weeks they'll feed 'em
sandlance, cod fry or capelin.
Then one morning the folks find themselves
all alone.

In the dark of the night,
not a predator in sight,
unfurling their wings, those chicks have
all flown.

In the early morning light of a late August day, Cid and Alice landed next to the young horned puffin couple.

"Hi neighbors. Did your chick fledge yet?" Cid asked.

"He left us sometime during the night. We've been looking for him but we can't find him anywhere," Al mourned.

"That's great!" said Cid cheerfully.

"GREAT? Cid, we've believed you about all kinds of things, but HOW...HOW can you think it's great that we can't find our chick?"

"It's all right, Al," said Alice. "It's great news, Cindy. It means that he escaped in the dark. It's the only way a chick can begin his life without becoming falcon food. Now your chick will float on the open ocean for three or more years. He will learn about the winds and the waves, about the seasons and about the fishes. Then one spring, as the days begin to get longer, he will grow glorious beak plates and beautiful horns. The rhythms of the earth will prepare a great adventure for him. Warmed by the sun's rays, the Japanese currents will surge north stirring the ocean's nutrients. Phytoplankton will bloom in the nutrient-rich-waters and the growing light. They will provide food for a great burst of growth among the zooplankton. The fishes will flourish on the zooplankton. Your chick will be a strong young puffin. He will heed the same call that draws all puffins back to the rookery. He will return like you did last spring to find a mate. The rich supplies of fishes will sustain him, his offspring and all of us. Why, if it weren't for puffins this place would be overrun with fish!

This is the great dance of life…
the way it is!

There have always been puffins."

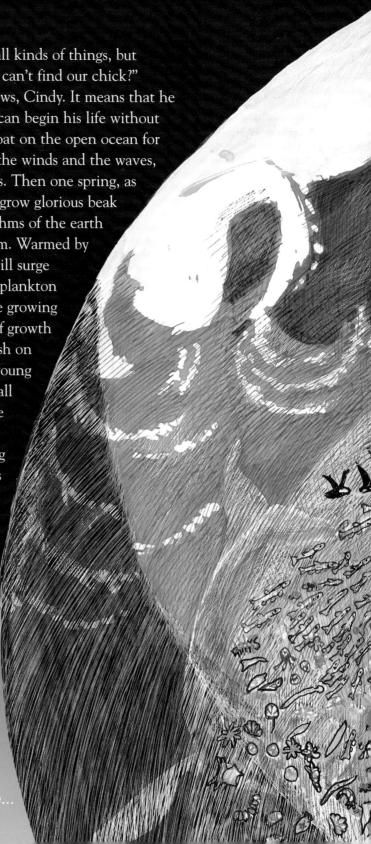

Pa puffins feel badly,
Ma puffins stare sadly,
at the place on their nests where those
 chicks used to be.

 But in truth it is good.
 The chicks did what they should.
 They are part of the great dance of life...
 and they're free.

There Have Always Been Puffins had its genesis over 40 years ago

when the oldest Rea sister, Robin, shared a poem she was learning in second grade with five-year-old Ba. Together they memorized the verse, as fledglings are known to do, and took it out to their own deep blue seas for thirty years.

Eventually, Robin and Ba reconstructed the rhyme to share with fledglings of their own. Ba illustrated the verse, as she and Robin had remembered it, and turned it into a cloth book for the infants of the family.

In the summer of 1996, the youngest Rea sister, C.J., was making regular trips aboard a tour boat to a puffin rookery in Alaska. She noticed that the park visitors were thrilled with the puffins. But there were few books available on puffins that were both informative and enjoyable. She called Ba and suggested a collaborative work that would include Florence's original poem.

For 6 months we generated ideas and researched the book. We were able to spend two weeks together in December of 1996. Born from the joy generated by Florence's simple verse, Al and Cid jumped into our lives, spun verses off Florence's rhyme and scrawled pictures across Ba's paper.

Though Florence's poem was in public domain, we wanted to truly thank her for her inspiration. We did some research and learned that Florence and her husband, Francis Lee Jaques, had spent their lifetimes writing about and illustrating the natural history of North America. Their books, written by Florence and accompanied by Francis Lee's exquisite scratch board artwork, are delightful. We are in awe of the footsteps in which we tread and wish to acknowledge Florence for starting it all, long before we were born.

After Florence, came a whole community of people who supported us in this endeavor. We wish to thank them all. Especially, we thank our father, Norman Rea. He believed in us, lent his financial backing, and gave us the advice we needed to get started and keep going. Our brother Mark turned the artwork into transparencies for printing production. Mindy and Jason King (Ba's kids) hunted for pictures, learned to cook their own meals and encouraged their mother even when her patience was short. Tara Chang offered great moral support and photographic files, an immense help in the illustration research. Bill Schiff worked painstakingly with the artwork and text, improving design and preparing the project for printing. He and the professional craftsmen at Schiff Printing helped us greatly with the mechanics and logistics of publishing and are responsible for the high quality printing of the book. We would also like to acknowledge Kenai Fjords Tours and Major Marine Tours who backed us, even before the printing was done, by purchasing large quantities of our book. Major Marine Tours' boat trips to the puffin rookery in the summer of 1996 gave C.J. the ideas for much of the natural history portion of the text. And finally we would like to thank Frank Anderson, Jim Allen and Oni Williams for editorial assistance.

C.J. and Ba Rea